D0228767

FishFace

Portraits by David Doubilet

Φ

Fish hate to have their picture taken. They dislike it even more than cats, birds, wild orang-utans or two-year-olds – a fish portraitist is an underwater oxymoron. It is virtually impossible to be a Karsh of the coral reef. Exquisite photographic moments in the sea are even more rare than those on land, and time underwater is constantly constrained by physics and physiology.

For humans, fish appear as alien creatures living in a weightless twilight world. For fish, human divers appear to be not just aliens but true monsters with giant blank, masked eyes and Medusa-like pipes sprouting from their heads, making violent bubbling noises.

When we do meet it is fleeting, but at times we are face to face, and I am looking into extraordinary turret eyes that see 180 degrees on each side of the fish's face. Then there are small moments when suddenly there seems to be an expression.

Fish are caricatures of humans – floating cartoons. Groupers look like everybody's Uncle Max and should be smoking cigars. Parrot fish, with their protruding teeth, all seem to be named Lou. The Red velvet fish from Tasmania has a swept back dorsal fin that resembles a pompadour, giving it an Elvis-like look. The Elephant fish looks like Eleanor Roosevelt or Margaret Thatcher.

There are crustaceans and turtles in this book as well as fish. I have included them because they share the same wonderful weightless expressions that fish have. And the variety is endless – from the nightmare-like faces of the Stargazer, to endearing faces like that of the Harlequin tusk fish with its tiny, bright blue, tusk-like teeth.

Most fish pictures show fish swimming away into the blue, but for a moment, in this book, they look at us.

David Doubilet

Red-lipped Caribbean bat fish, Isle of Youth, Cuba, 2000

4

Cookie cutter shark, Suruga Bay, Japan, 1979

Blenny, Poor Knights Islands, New Zealand, 1987
Overleaf: Black cod and shipwreck, Middleton Reef, Australia, 1987

Yellowmargin moray eel and Cleaner shrimp,
Mabul, Malaysia, 1996
Overleaf: Bumphead wrasse, Red Sea, Israel, 1980

17

Long-nosed weed fish, Tasmania, Australia, 1995
Overleaf: Porcupine fish, Red Sea, Israel, 1982

Yellow puffer fish, Aldabra Atoll, Seychelles, 1993

23

New Zealand rock lobster, Doubtful Sound,
New Zealand, 1986

Saw shark, Tasmania, Australia, 1995

24

Spine-cheeked anemone fish, Kimbe Bay,
Papua New Guinea, 1997

Red and black anemone fish, Milne Bay, Papua New Guinea, 1997

Great barracuda, Little Cayman Island, 1999

Yellow angler fish, Izu, Japan, 1989
Overleaf: Bicolour parrot fish, Red Sea, Egypt, 1991

37

Unicorn fish, Red Sea, Israel, 1974
Overleaf: Blue-barred parrot fish, Sipadan Island,
Malaysia, 1997

Swell shark, Channel Islands, California, USA, 1996
Overleaf: Silky shark, Gardens of the Queen, Cuba, 2000

Midas blenny, Red Sea, Israel, 1985

Fringehead blenny, Izu, Japan, 1981
Overleaf: Crocodile fish, Yap Island, Micronesia, 1992

51

Pig fish, Stewart Island, New Zealand, 1987

Overleaf: Diagonal-banded sweetlips and Cleaner wrasse, Great Barrier Reef, Australia, 1999

Sargassum angler fish, Kungkungan Bay,
Indonesia, 2001
Overleaf: Tomato grouper, Kimbe Bay,
Papua New Guinea, 1997

Narrow-lined cardinal fish, Bali, Indonesia, 1997
Overleaf: Puffer fish, Aldabra Atoll, Seychelles, 1992

Earspot angel fish, Aldabra Atoll, Seychelles, 1993

Bumphead parrot fish, Sipadan Island, Malaysia, 1997
Overleaf: Bumphead parrot fish, Sipadan Island,
Malaysia, 1997

Blue-spotted grouper and Cleaner wrasse,
Great Barrier Reef, Australia, 1989

Giant Japanese spider crab, Izu, Japan, 1989
Overleaf: Hermit crab, Cayo Largo, Cuba, 2000

Arrow crab, Grand Cayman Island, 1984
Overleaf: Wolf eel, Vancouver Island, Canada, 1979

Black-spotted moray eel, Djibouti, East Africa, 1992
Overleaf: Japanese tora (tiger) moray eel, Izu, Japan, 1984

82

Yellow-masked angel fish, New Ireland,
Papua New Guinea, 1987
Overleaf: Mantis shrimp, Bali, Indonesia, 1997

Potato-faced angler fish, Kungkungan Bay, Indonesia, 2001

Yellow hairy angler fish, Milne Bay,
Papua New Guinea, 1994

Spotted snake eel, Suruga Bay, Japan, 1989

94

Snake eel, Suruga Bay, Japan, 1989
Overleaf: Pacific moray eel and Red shrimp,
Channel Islands, California, USA, 1985

Pacific moray eel and Red shrimp, Channel Islands, California, USA, 1985

Blackspot angel fish, Kimbe Bay,
Papua New Guinea, 1996
Overleaf: Blue ribbon eel, Milne Bay,
Papua New Guinea, 1994

Zebra lion fish, Flores, Indonesia, 1997
Overleaf: Wolf eel and Sea urchin, Vancouver Island, Canada, 1980

Lord Howe Island hawk fish, Australia, 1987
Overleaf: White-eyed moray eels, Shark Bay,
Western Australia, 1989

Harlequin tusk fish, Great Barrier Reef, Australia, 1999

114

Sponge crab, Shark Bay, Western Australia, 1989
Overleaf: Tiger shark, Aliwal Shoals, South Africa, 2003

Marbled snake eel, Milne Bay, Papua New Guinea, 1997

120

Sea robin, Tasmania, Australia, 1998
Overleaf: Snake eel, Milne Bay,
Papua New Guinea, 1986

Potbellied sea horse, Tasmania, Australia, 1995

129

Green turtle and Juvenile wrasse, Great Barrier Reef,
Australia, 1989
Overleaf: Long-nosed hawk fish, Bali, Indonesia, 1996

Ziebell's hand fish, Tasmania, Australia, 1995
Overleaf: Ziebell's hand fish, Tasmania, Australia, 1995

Cow fish, Tasmania, Australia, 1995
Overleaf: Sea moth (pegasus), Flores, Indonesia, 1996

Mandarin fish, Koror, Palau, 1994
Overleaf: Weedy sea dragon, Tasmania, Australia, 199

145

Mating Loggerhead turtles, Florida Keys, USA, 1998
Overleaf: Mating Loggerhead turtles, Florida Keys, USA, 1998

Meyer's butterfly fish, Kimbe Bay,
Papua New Guinea, 1986
Overleaf: Scorpion fish, Poor Knights Islands,
New Zealand, 1986

153

Potato cod and Cleaner wrasse, Great Barrier Reef, Australia, 1989

Overleaf: Potato cod and Cleaner wrasse, Great Barrier Reef, Australia, 1989

Hawk fish, Izu, Japan, 1982

Reef cuttle fish, Great Barrier Reef, Australia, 1999

Reef cuttle fish, Great Barrier Reef, Australia, 1999
Overleaf: Rhinopias scorpion fish, Milne Bay,
Papua New Guinea, 1996

165

Pipe fish, Mabul, Malaysia, 1996
Overleaf: Angler fish, Izu, Japan, 1981

Red hand fish, Tasmania, Australia, 1995

Overleaf: A pair of Red hand fish, Tasmania, Australia, 1995

173

Pygmy sea horses, Kungkungan Bay, Indonesia, 200□
Overleaf: Stargazer, Kungkungan Bay, Indonesia, 20□

177

Jaw fish, Cayo Largo, Cuba, 2000
Overleaf: Bandtooth conger eel, Isle of Youth,
Cuba, 2000

Cow fish, Tasmania, Australia, 1995

183

Yellow hamlet, Cayo Largo, Cuba, 2000
Overleaf: Giant cuttle fish, Tasmania, Australia, 1995

Randall's shrimp goby, Bali, Indonesia, 1996
Overleaf: Spotted hawk fish, Galapagos Islands,
Ecuador, 1998

Whip coral goby, Great Barrier Reef, Australia, 1999
Overleaf: Leafy sea dragon, Adelaide,
South Australia, 1984

195

Bicolour blenny, Great Barrier Reef, Australia, 1989
Overleaf: Weed fish, Ewens Ponds,
South Australia, 1981

199

Yellowmouth moray eel, Aliwal Shoals,
South Africa, 2002
Overleaf: Rhinopias scorpion fish, Milne Bay,
Papua New Guinea, 1996

Garibaldi fish, Channel Islands, California, USA, 1997
Overleaf: Flowery flounder, Kungkungan Bay,
Indonesia, 2001

Striped morwong, South Australia, 1984
Overleaf: Morwong, Lord Howe Island, Australia, 1987

Lizard fish eating a False cleaner wrasse,
Espirito Santo Island, Vanuatu, 1986
Overleaf: Stoplight parrot fish in sleeping bubble,
Grand Cayman Island, 1984

Spinyhead blenny, Cayo Largo, Cuba, 2000
Overleaf: Great white shark, Gansbaai,
South Africa, 1999

Great white shark, Gansbaai, South Africa, 2001

Tomato clown fish, Kimbe Bay,
Papua New Guinea, 1996

Swimmer crab and Shrimp in coral, Mabul,
Malaysia, 1996

Mantis shrimp, Flores, Indonesia, 1996
Overleaf: Flying gurnard, Kungkungan Bay, Indonesia, 2001

Ragged-tooth sharks, Aliwal Shoals, South
Overleaf: Ragged-tooth shark, Aliwal Shoa
South Africa, 2001

Red and black anemone fish,
Milne Bay, Papua New Guinea, 1996
Overleaf: Southern stingray,
Grand Cayman Island, 1986

Red-lipped Caribbean bat fish, Isle of Youth, Cuba, 2000
Overleaf: Octopus and diver, Cayo Largo, Cuba, 2000

For Jennifer

US photographer David Doubilet has been snorkelling since the age of eight. At thirteen he started taking his first underwater photographs in the green sea off the New Jersey coast and published his first pictures in *National Geographic* in 1972. He is widely acclaimed as one of the world's leading underwater photographers and has reported on most of the world's oceans, covering everything from shipwrecks to sharks. He is a contributing photographer in residence at the National Geographic Society, an honorary fellow of the Royal Photographic Society, and has won many awards including the Lennart Nilsson Award in 2001. His other publications include *Water Light Time* (1999), also published by Phaidon Press.

Index

Phaidon Press Limited
Regent's Wharf
All Saints Street
London N1 9PA

Phaidon Press Inc.
180 Varick Street
New York, NY 10014

www.phaidon.com

First published 2003
© 2003 Phaidon Press Limited
Photographs and text © 2003 David Doubilet

ISBN 0 7148 4301 6

Designed by Untitled
Printed in China

Harlequin tusk fish, Great Barrier Reef, Australia, 1999
Overleaf: Reef squid, Isle of Youth, Cuba, 2000

Monkey-faced scorpion fish, Flores, Indonesia, 1996
Overleaf: Stone fish, Great Barrier Reef, Australia, 1999

Glass-eye snapper, Grand Cayman Island, 1984
Overleaf: Sea horse, Izu, Japan, 1982

219

Red Irish lord, Vancouver Island, Canada, 1980
Overleaf: Tongue sole, Kungkungan Bay,
Indonesia, 2001

Yellow-headed jaw fish with eggs, Cayo Largo, Cuba, 2000
Overleaf: Red velvet fish, Tasmania, Australia, 1995

Semicircle angel fish, Kimbe Bay, Papua New Guinea, 1995

Soft coral goby, Bali, Indonesia, 1996

Sweetlips and Cleaner wrasse, Astove Atoll, Seychelles, 1993

Overleaf: Blue-striped grunts, Florida Keys, USA, 1997

Barramundi cod, Great Barrier Reef, Australia, 1999

234

Giant squirrel fish, Peleliu Island, Palau, 2003
Overleaf: Porcupine fish, Grand Cayman Island, 1984

Snowflake moray eel, Great Barrier Reef, Australia, 2000

Overleaf: Elephant fish, Tasmania, Australia, 1995

245

Steamer wrasse, Galapagos Islands, Ecuador, 1998
Overleaf: Toad fish, Exmouth, Western Australia, 2002

Flowery cod, Great Barrier Reef, Australia, 1999

Blenny, Poor Knights Islands, New Zealand, 1986
Overleaf: Flashlight fish, Eilat, Israel, 1977

Goby on Elephant ear sponge, Bali, Indonesia, 1996
Overleaf: Stinging cat fish, Lord Howe Island,
Australia, 1986

Snake eel, Kungkungan Bay, Indonesia, 2001
Overleaf: Spiny porcupine fish, Suruga Bay, Japan, 1989

Dragonet fish, Suruga Bay, Japan, 1989
Overleaf: Nassau grouper and Cleaner goby,
Cayo Largo, Cuba, 2000

Diagonal-banded sweetlips and Cleaner wrasse, Bali, Indonesia, 1996
Overleaf: Nine-lined sweetlips, Aldabra Atoll, Seychelles, 1992

Longfin bat fish, Sipadan Island, Malaysia, 1996

Inimicus scorpion fish, Kungkungan Bay,
Indonesia, 2001
Overleaf: Inimicus scorpion fish, Kungkungan Bay,
Indonesia, 2001

Squarespot anthias, German Channel, Palau, 1996
Overleaf: Orangespine unicorn fish, Milne Bay,
Papua New Guinea, 1996

Leaf scorpion fish, Manado, Indonesia, 1995
Overleaf: Spotted scorpion fish, Lighthouse Reef, Belize, 2002

Clown anemone fish, Milne Bay,
Papua New Guinea, 1996
Overleaf: Blue trigger fish and Cleaner wrasse,
Red Sea, Israel, 1977

Titan trigger fish, Red Sea, Israel, 1985
Overleaf: Whale shark, North Cape,
Western Australia, 1992

Hawk-faced moray eel, Astove Atoll, Seychelles, 1993
Overleaf: Great barracuda, Little Cayman Island, 1999

Tarpon, Grand Cayman Island, 1999

Red-spotted hawk fish, Hawaii, USA, 1985
Overleaf: Manta ray, Hawaii, USA, 1994

Box crab, Saba, Netherlands Antilles, 2002
Overleaf: Stargazer, Red Sea, Israel, 1981

French angel fish, Grand Cayman Island, 1985
Overleaf: French angel fish, Grand Cayman Island, 1985

Orange anemone fish, Russell Islands,
Solomon Islands, 1986
Overleaf: Sculpin, Tasmania, Australia, 1995

315

Sharp-tailed snake eel, St Lucia, 1979
Overleaf: Star puffer fish, Bora Bora,
French Polynesia, 1995

Chambered nautilus, Manus Island,
Papua New Guinea, 1987
Overleaf: Lizard fish, Bali, Indonesia, 1996

Blue-spotted grouper, Kimbe Bay,
Papua New Guinea, 1996
Overleaf: Banded goby, Flores, Indonesia, 1996

327

Banded goby, Flores, Indonesia, 1996
Overleaf: Cabezon, Monterey, California, USA, 1989

Venus (anchor) tusk fish, Great Barrier Reef, Australia, 1999

Overleaf: Japanese scorpion fish, Izu, Japan, 1981

Clown snake eel, Bali, Indonesia, 1996
Overleaf: Jew fish, Grand Cayman Island, 1986

Mottled moray eel, Kungkungan Bay, Indonesia, 2001
Overleaf: Red Sea coral grouper, Brothers Islands,
Egypt, 1991

Urchin puffer fish, False Bay, South Africa, 2001
Overleaf: Octopus, False Bay, South Africa, 2001

Hotlips tripplefin, False Bay, South Africa, 2001
Overleaf: Blue shark, California, USA, 1979

Pinnate bat fish, Kungkungan Bay, Indonesia, 2001
Overleaf: Barbed-mouth fish, False Bay,
South Africa, 2001

Map puffer fish, Great Barrier Reef, Australia, 1999
Overleaf: Stars and stripes puffer fish and Shrimp,
Great Barrier Reef, Australia, 1999

Beaked leather jacket, Kungkungan Bay, Indonesia, 2001
Overleaf: Reef squid, Isle of Youth, Cuba, 2000

Pike blenny, Cayo Largo, Cuba, 2000
Overleaf: Slipper lobster, Kungkungan Bay,
Indonesia, 2001

Yellow damsel fish, Great Barrier Reef, Australia, 1999